KAUNAS LITHUANIA Travel Guide

Unlock Hidden Gems, Must-See Sights, Culture, Adventures, and Thrilling Experiences"

Cori J. Smith

Copyright© Cori J. Smith 2024

Table of Contents

INTRODUCTION

Salutations to everybody, fellow tourists, and salutations from the lovely city of Kaunas! Lithuania's second-largest city, Kaunas, lies tucked away along the banks of the Nemunas River and is a hidden gem just waiting to be explored. Kaunas promises an amazing adventure with its rich history, lively culture, and flawless fusion of medieval and modern influences.

The charming scenery and storied architecture of Kaunas will welcome you with open arms. Discover the mysteries of the city's Old Town, which has well-preserved houses and cobblestone streets. As you go down Liberty Avenue, a busy road brimming with stores, cafes, and the vibrancy of the locals, you can feel the pulse of Kaunas.

Explore the meeting point of innovation and tradition in the center of Kaunas. From the striking Kaunas Castle, which has stood tall since the fourteenth century, to the modern art galleries scattered across the city, Kaunas skillfully unites its fascinating history with its vibrant present.

In Kaunas, your adventure commences not only with geographical investigation but also with an absorption into the essence of the city. Participate in chats with the people in their preferred cafés, and observe how the city reveals its distinct personality. With wide arms, Kaunas greets you and promises an adventure full of beauty, surprises, and a sense of community.

An Overview of Travel Destinations to Kaunas

Let's explore what makes Kaunas such a fascinating place to visit. Kaunas is located in the geographic center of Lithuania, at 54.8985° N latitude and 23.9036° E longitude. Because of its advantageous position, you can easily visit not only the city but also the nearby historic sites and natural beauties.

Kaunas has an impressive collection of buildings representing a wide range of architectural styles. A living reminder of the city's rich past is the Old Town, which features elements from the Gothic, Renaissance, and Baroque periods. Concurrently, contemporary constructions such as the Vytautas the Great Bridge demonstrate Kaunas's dedication to advancement.

This city is a cultural oasis rather than merely a sight to behold. For those looking for intellectual stimulation, Kaunas is a veritable gold mine with its abundance of museums, art galleries, and theaters. Visit the Maironis Lithuanian Literature Museum to learn about Lithuanian literature, or visit the Vytautas the Great War Museum to see the turbulent history of the nation.

You'll feel the genuine kindness of Kaunas's people as you stroll through its streets. The people who live there are proud of their city and want to tell tourists about its history and customs. Get ready to lose yourself in the vibrant ambiance of the neighborhood markets, where the scent of authentic Lithuanian food fills the air.

Why Kaunas?

"Why choose Kaunas for my next adventure?" you may be asking yourself now. The city's distinctive fusion of culture, history, and modern vibrancy holds the key to the solution.

When compared to major cities in Europe, Kaunas provides a more personal experience. Because of the slow pace, you may enjoy each moment without feeling hurried. It's a place where you may take strolls through the Old Town's winding streets, uncovering hidden treasures at every turn, or where you can unwind by the serene Kaunas Reservoir.

Another strong point is Kaunas's affordability. Reasonably priced lodging, food, and entertainment make it a great choice for tourists on a tight budget. Kaunas is kind to the economy, but it doesn't skimp on the caliber of experiences it provides.

Kaunas offers a wealth of cultural enrichment to those who seek it. The city's many festivals, which feature anything from avant-garde acts to classical music, demonstrate its dedication to the arts. Take part in a traditional folk festival, become fully immersed in the local way of life, and see how proud the people of Kaunas are of their heritage.

Kaunas is more than just a place to visit; it's an invitation to discover, educate yourself, and become enthralled with a city that embraces the future while holding fast to its past. Whether you're a history buff, an art lover, or someone looking for a relaxed getaway, Kaunas extends a warm welcome and promises an extraordinary experience.

History of Kaunas

With origins in the Middle Ages, Kaunas has experienced the ups and downs of history, molding it into the vibrant metropolis that it is today. Originally a timber castle, Kaunas was founded in the eleventh century and developed into a major commercial station along the Nemunas River.

After Kaunas Castle was built in the fourteenth century and came to represent tenacity and strength, the city's stature grew. Kaunas has seen fires, invasions, and changing political environments over the ages, symbolizing the ups and downs of Lithuania.

During the early 1900s, Kaunas took over as Lithuania's temporary capital while Vilnius was ruled by Poland.

Known as the "interwar" years, these years had a lasting impact on the city. The functionalist-style structures from that era's architecture attest to Kaunas's significance throughout this pivotal period.

Nazi Germany and the Soviet Union both occupied Kaunas while the Second World War raged. Although the war left its scars, Kaunas recovered from it, rebuilding and regaining its identity. More changes followed the war, transforming the city into one of the Soviet Union's most active industrial and cultural centers.

Following Lithuania's return to independence in 1991, Kaunas carried on with its makeover. The city's famous past is still felt in its streets and sites today, enticing tourists to discover the many facets of its rich history.

Kaunas Culture

Kaunas is a cultural mosaic that skillfully combines the old and the new. The rich legacy of literature, art, and folklore in the city is the foundation of a thriving cultural environment.

Art and Architecture: Kaunas's architectural legacy is exhibited in the Old Town, which features Gothic, Baroque, and Renaissance structures. Institutions such as the M. K. Čiurlionis National Art Museum, which honors the compositions and artwork of Lithuania's renowned artists, are spaces where modern art may be found.

Museums: With institutions like the Devil's Museum and the Vytautas the Great War Museum, which provide insights into the nation's wartime experiences and folklore, Kaunas is a sanctuary for history buffs.

Festivals: The city comes alive with a plethora of festivals honoring anything from modern art to classical music and cinema. Notable events that draw in both residents and tourists from abroad are the Pažaislis

Music Festival and the Kaunas Jazz Festival.

Literature: The Maironis Lithuanian Literature Museum, devoted to conserving and advancing the nation's literary legacy, is located in Kaunas, a city with a rich literary culture. The literary masterpieces of Lithuania are available for exploration.

Folk Traditions: Go to a traditional folk festival to get a true sense of Kaunas culture. These gatherings offer a window into Lithuania's culture through the colorful costumes, melodies, and dances that have been passed down through the ages.

Local Cuisine: Those who are keen to discover Kaunas's culinary scene are in for a treat. With a range of options from inventive modern food to hearty traditional dishes, the city's restaurants showcase a varied palette shaped by its topography and history.

Kaunas, a compelling Lithuanian city, welcomes you to interact with its stories, immerse yourself in its art, and enjoy the distinct fusion of history and modern vibrancy. Its historical resilience and cultural richness make it an unforgettable experience.

CHAPTER 1

Getting Started

Essential Travel Information

Greetings, brave visitors! Join us as we walk you through the essential information required for a smooth journey in Kaunas. Now let's get into the vital travel knowledge that will make your trip more enjoyable and trouble-free.

Getting Around: The center of Kaunas is easily accessible after landing at Kaunas International Airport (KUN), which is about 14 kilometers from the city center. There are plenty of taxis and airport shuttles that may take you to your lodging in a comfortable manner.

Once in the city, getting around is easy. Buses and trolleybuses are part of Kaunas' public transit fleet, which makes getting around the city and its environs simple. If you want a more customized experience, think about hiring a bicycle or taking a leisurely walk throughout the Old Town's quaint streets.

Money and Banking: The Euro (€) is the official currency of Lithuania. There are numerous ATMs located across Kaunas, along with a reputable banking system, making cash withdrawals easy. While most restaurants, hotels, and other larger facilities accept credit cards, it's a good idea to have extra cash on hand for smaller vendors and local markets.

Language basics: Although English is commonly spoken in tourist areas, Lithuanian is the official language. Acquiring a few fundamental Lithuanian words can be a fun approach to improving your cultural experience and establishing connections with locals. But don't worry, during your visit, communication won't be a problem.

Health and Safety Advice: Due to its low crime rate, Kaunas is a safe city for visitors. Nevertheless, it's crucial to maintain awareness and exercise common sense, including watching out for your possessions in busy places. The police, ambulance, and fire services emergency number is 112.

Medical institutions in Kaunas are conveniently accessible and provide high-quality healthcare. Make sure your travel insurance includes coverage for unforeseen medical crises. You may stay hydrated in Kaunas without worrying because the tap water is safe to consume.

Local Protocol: The Kaunas community is renowned for its warmth and kindness. A firm handshake is customary for greetings, however, a simple "Labas" (hello) will do just fine.

It's polite to take off your shoes when you visit someone's house.

Tipping is not required in restaurants, however it is appreciated. A generous tip is ten percent. It is recommended to dress modestly when visiting places of worship such as churches. Your interactions with the locals will only be improved by embracing these cultural quirks.

Now that you are equipped with these crucial data, let's discuss when is the best time to visit Kaunas so you can discover its hidden gems.

Best Times to Visit

As picking the ideal time to visit Kaunas can greatly affect your experience, let's discover the secrets of each season and assist you in making that decision.

Spring (April to June): Kaunas blossoms into a tapestry of colors when the weather warms. Parks and gardens come to life in the spring, which is the perfect season to observe nature's rebirth. The weather is favorable for outdoor activities, with mild to warm temperatures. This is the ideal time of year to explore parks like Santakos Park, take walks through the Old Town, and go to local festivals.

Summer (July through August): This is when Kaunas is most radiant. This is the busiest travel season, with long daylight hours and temperatures between 18°C and 25°C (64°F and 77°F). The city holds a lot of events, including outdoor concerts and festivals. Take advantage of the chance to unwind by the Kaunas Reservoir or experience a beautiful view of the city from a hot air balloon flight.

Autumn (September to November): Autumn brings a symphony of warm hues to Kaunas as summer ends. The range of temperatures drops to 5°C to 15°C (41°F to 59°F). For those looking for a more sedate and less crowded experience, now is the ideal time of year. Take a stroll along the riverbanks to see the changing colors of Pazaislis Monastery's surroundings and enjoy the cool air.

Winter (December to March): During the winter, Kaunas creates a magnificent ambiance by dressing in a calm covering of snow. Even though it can get as low as -5°C (23°F), the city transforms into a winter paradise. For those who love snow-dusted Old Town, warm cafes, and lively markets, winter is a great time of year. Enjoy the comfort of regional food at classic pubs or skate on the ice rink in Town Hall Square.

When organizing your trip to Kaunas, take into account your interests, such as whether you're drawn to the vibrant summer festivals, the peaceful autumn scenery, or the captivating winter vistas. Every season reveals a different aspect of the city, so your experience will be customized to your preferences. Your trip to Kaunas is set to begin now that you know when to visit and the needed travel information.

How to Reach Kaunas

Starting your journey via Kaunas? Together, we will find the best paths and solutions to get you to this energetic Lithuanian city.

By Air: Your point of entry into Kaunas is the Kaunas International Airport (KUN), which is situated about 14 kilometers from the city center. It provides a handy entrance point for visitors from outside Europe, connecting to several European locations. Taxis and shuttle services are easily accessible from the airport, offering convenient transportation to your lodging.

The cost of your flight varies based on when you book and where you depart. Taxis and shuttle services are easily accessible from the airport. While shuttle services may cost between 8 and 12 euros per person, a cab ride to the city center may cost between 15 and 20 euros.

By Train: Kaunas has excellent train connections, making travel there quick and enjoyable. Kaunas Railway Station, the city's principal train station, is situated in the middle of the area. Kaunas is connected by direct trains to important cities such as Vilnius, Klaipėda, and Šiauliai. The train ride is inexpensive, and comfortable, and offers a view of Lithuania's rural areas. An affordable and picturesque way to get to Kaunas is by train. The class and kind of train determine the cost of the tickets. A second-class ticket from Vilnius to Kaunas, for instance, may run you between 10 and 15 euros. The train station is well situated, and a trip to your lodging from the station can cost between one and two euros by public transit.

By Bus: Kaunas is connected to nearby cities and nations via a vast bus network. One important hub is the Kaunas Bus Station, which is ideally located close to the Old Town. Whether traveling from Warsaw, Riga, or Vilnius, buses offer a practical and affordable mode of transportation. An affordable way to get to Kaunas is by bus. The bus company and distance have an impact on the cost. A bus ticket from Riga to Kaunas, for example, may run you between 20 and 30 euros. The bus terminal is in a handy location, and buses can cost between one and two euros for local travel within the city.

By Car: Renting a car is a good choice if you want the independence of the open road. Because of Lithuania's well-maintained roads, traveling from Vilnius to Kaunas takes about one and a half hours. Enjoy the freedom to take your time exploring the stunning scenery, and don't forget to become familiar with the local traffic laws and signage. The flexibility of renting a car comes at a price, though, as there are gasoline charges, rental fees, and even tolls. Rental costs vary based on the type of automobile and rental company and can range from 20 to 50 euros per day. A liter of fuel costs between 1.30 and 1.50 euros. There may be tolls on some roads.

You've made it to Kaunas, now let's look at your alternatives for getting around the city.

Transportation within the City

With so many different modes of transportation available, Kaunas is easy to navigate and provides flexibility for discovering the city's hidden gems.

Public Transit: The effective public transit system in Kaunas consists of buses and trolleybuses. Numerous sights are easily accessible because of the highways that traverse both the city and its environs. Get a magnetic card, add credit to it, and travel through Kaunas without difficulty. Check the timetables beforehand because taking public transportation can be a great way to meet people in the area and find hidden treasures. In Kaunas, public transportation is reasonably priced. For between 1.50 and

2 euros, you may get a magnetic card for buses and trolleybuses. Typically, a single ticket costs one euro for a single journey. For frequent passengers, weekly or monthly passes offer further savings.

Cycling: Renting a bicycle can make your exploration more environmentally friendly and athletic. With dedicated bike lanes, Kaunas is a bike-friendly city where you can ride your bike around the Old Town or along the picturesque riverbanks. There are lots of bike rental options that offer a fun way to explore the charms of the city. Bicycle rentals are an inexpensive and environmentally beneficial choice. The cost of renting a bike is between five and ten euros per day. Additionally, a lot of rental companies provide hourly prices, so you may adjust the price to fit your exploration schedule.

Walking: Kaunas is a great city to explore on foot because of its small size and quaint Old Town. Put on some comfy shoes and explore the winding cobblestone streets, where you'll come across interesting street art, quaint cafes, and historical sites. You can take your time taking in the atmosphere of the city while strolling around and discovering surprises at every turn.

Taxis: Kaunas has an abundance of taxis, making them a practical choice for people who need door-to-door transportation. Taxis are dependable, secure, and flexible, particularly if you need to get to certain locations quickly. Make sure the taxi is using a meter, or decide on the fare before you get in. In Kaunas, taxi fares are fairly priced. Usually, the first ticket is between two and three euros, and there are additional fees every kilometer. A quick ride within the city might cost between 5 and 10 euros, whilst a trip outside the city might cost between 15 and 20 euros.

Car Rentals: Kaunas offers a wide selection of car rentals if you'd rather travel in comfort in your vehicle. You can easily travel throughout the city and its environs when you have a car. Observe parking laws and take advantage of the freedom to personalize your schedule.

The type of vehicle and length of the rental both affect the cost of a car hire. The cost of a day's rental might vary from 20 to 50 euros. Depending on how far you have to travel, fuel costs could add up to an extra 10 to 20 euros a day.

Explore Kaunas's varied neighborhoods, historic monuments, and natural beauties via its well-connected transit alternatives. Whether you opt for the convenience of public transportation, the liberty of cycling, or the luxury of a cab, your trip around Kaunas is sure to be as enjoyable as the places you get to see.

CHAPTER 2

Unlocking Hidden Gems

Lesser-Known Neighborhoods

Hikers, welcome to the undiscovered areas of Kaunas where the beating heart of the city can be heard in less well-known districts. Discover the true spirit of Kaunas by exploring these pockets of authenticity, while the Old Town enchants with its well-traveled alleyways.

Žaliakalnis: With a peaceful ambiance and panoramic views of the Old Town,

Žaliakalnis is nestled on the hillsides. Take a stroll down the residential streets that feature buildings from the Art Deco and Functionalism periods. Be sure not to overlook the Žaliakalnis Funicular Railway, which links the neighborhood's top and lower sections at Vytauto Avenue. Address: 44 Vytauto Avenue, Kaunas, Lithuania 44297.

Aleksotas: The quaint neighborhood of Aleksotas is located across the Nemunas River. Take a stroll down Maironio Street, which is renowned for its vibrant wooden homes and creative atmosphere. Explore the historic Aleksotas Funicular Railway, which links Aleksotas and the Old Town.
Maironio G., 28, 44298 Kaunas, Lithuania is the address. Funicular hours: daily from 6:30 am to 10 pm. Price: About one euro.

Dainava: This area, renowned for its cultural richness, invites you to embrace the local way of life. Discover the thriving Taikos Avenue market, which offers a wide variety of tastes and customs. A calm getaway, Dainava Park is ideal for a stroll.

Address: 51122 Kaunas, Lithuania, Taikos Avenue, 73.

Baltasis Fortas: Visit Baltasis Fortas, a residential area featuring the ruins of a 19th-century fortification, to travel back in time. Explore the charming wooden cottages that have withstood the test of time as you meander along the winding streets. Address: Kaunas, Lithuania; Baltasis Fortas.

Vilijampolė: Despite having an industrial heritage, Vilijampolė is today a refuge for bohemians. Discover the rich, varied plant collections of the Kaunas Botanical Garden. The Kaunas Photography Gallery, which features the creations of regional and worldwide artists, is also located in the neighborhood. Maironio G., 43, 44249 Kaunas, Lithuania is the address of the botanical garden. Opening times: daily from 8 a.m. to 6 p.m. Expenses: About two euros.

Eiguliai: With its suburban appeal and leisure areas, Eiguliai entices. See the Kaunas Lagoon, a calm reservoir encircled by vegetation that's perfect for a leisurely afternoon. The Aleksotas Observation Deck, which offers breathtaking city views, is another feature of the neighborhood. Address: Ąžuolyno g., 14, 47191 Kaunas, Lithuania (Kaunas Lagoon). Maironio g., 28, 44298 Kaunas, Lithuania is the address of the observation deck. Opening times: daily from 10 a.m. to 8 p.m. Expenses: About two euros.

Babuskinskės: A neighborhood renowned for its cultural richness, Babuškinskės is worth exploring off the usual tourist path. Take a look at the distinctive sculptures created by regional artists in the Babtynas Sculpture Park, an outdoor exhibition. Address: Karaliaus Mindaugo pr (Babtynas Sculpture Park). 51, Kaunas, Lithuania 44334.

Off-the-Beaten-Path Attractions

Through off-the-beaten-path attractions, Kaunas unveils its hidden treasures, where natural wonders, art, and history come together to surprise and enchant visitors.

Kaunas Ninth Fort: The Ninth Fort honors the victims of Nazi atrocities and serves as a grim reflection of history. Discover the dark sides of World War II in the museum housed within the fort. Address: Žemaičių pl., 73, 44329 Kaunas, Lithuania. Opening times: Tuesday through Sunday, 9 a.m. to 5 p.m. Price: About four euros.

Kaunas Interwar Architecture Museum: Explore the architectural development of Kaunas at the Kaunas Interwar Architecture Museum. Located in the distinctive White Swan building, it provides a glimpse into the changes that the city underwent between the wars. Maironio G., 9, 44298 Kaunas, Lithuania is the address. Hours of operation: Tuesday through Sunday, 11 a.m. to 7 p.m. Expense: About two euros.

Abandoned Military Bunker in Aleksotas: The abandoned military bunker in Aleksotas provides a window into Kaunas's military past for those who enjoy urban exploration. For individuals who are interested in historical relics, it's a fascinating sight that's close to Zanavykų Street.

Ciurlionis Tunnel: The Ciurlionis Tunnel is an underpass decorated with colorful murals that blend art and urban space. It gives your trip through Kaunas a burst of color and is close to the Vytautas the Great Church. Maironio G., 20, 44298 Kaunas, Lithuania is the address.

Underground Printing House: Explore the world of underground printing at this establishment. This undiscovered treasure, tucked under Kaunas' streets, was vital to the Soviet Union. Tours led by guides shed light on its covert activities. Rotušės a., 19, 44298 Kaunas, Lithuania is the address. By appointment, tours are offered.

Maironis Lithuanian Literature Museum Garden: The garden of the Maironis Lithuanian Literature Museum is a calm haven away from the literary treasures housed within. Decorated with artwork and foliage, it provides a tranquil haven right in the middle of the Old Town. Rotušės a., 13, 44298 Kaunas, Lithuania is the address.

Devil's Museum: Explore the bizarre universe of this collection of artwork and artifacts depicting the devil. Situated on Maironio Street, it features a collection of international depictions of the devil. Maironio G., 6, 44298 Kaunas, Lithuania is the address. Hours of operation: Wednesday through Sunday, 11 a.m. to 5 p.m. Price: About three euros.

Explore these lesser-known areas and off-the-beaten-path attractions in Kaunas to start your adventure of discovery. Discover the city's varied fabric by venturing outside the often traveled routes; every corner reveals a tale, a fragment of history, or an artistic revelation.

Local Hangouts and Cafés

Greetings, friends who enjoy shady nooks and fragrant beverages! Through local hangouts that serve more than just coffee, but also a taste of the local way of life, Kaunas, Lithuania, reveals its thriving café culture. Discover seven cozy cafés where you may enjoy a drink, nibble on some food, and take in all of Kaunas's beauty.

Nemunas Island Café: Nestled on the scenic Nemunas Island, this café provides a peaceful haven amidst the natural surroundings. Savor your coffee outside on the patio overlooking the river. Nemunas Island, Kaunas, Lithuania is the address.

Miesto Kavinė: Nestled in the center of the Old Town, Miesto Kavinė radiates a classic charm. The diverse décor and mismatched furniture provide the impression of walking into a comfortable living area. Maironio G., 9, 44298 Kaunas, Lithuania is the address.

Kačių Kavinė (Cat Café): Cat lovers can have a distinctive experience at Kačių Kavinė (Cat Café). Savor your coffee in a comfortable, feline-friendly setting while surrounded by lively cats. Maironio G., 2, 44298 Kaunas, Lithuania is the address. Opening times: Monday through Sunday, 10 a.m. to 8 p.m.

Monkafe: Located in the center of Žaliakalnis, Monkafe entices with its tasteful decor and emphasis on premium coffee. This hidden gem in the area is well-known for its calm atmosphere and expertly crafted drinks. Maironio G., 28, 44298 Kaunas, Lithuania is the address.

Zoofari Coffee Roasters: Coffee enthusiasts will find paradise at Zoofari Coffee Roasters, a specialized coffee store where they roast their coffee beans. There is a wonderful atmosphere created by the aroma of freshly ground coffee filling the air. Kęstučio g., 26, 44298 Kaunas, Lithuania is the address.

Ponios Alus: Combining a warm café atmosphere with a passion for craft beer, Ponios Alus offers more than just coffee. It's the ideal place for anyone looking for a laid-back evening because it serves a variety of domestic and foreign beers. Maironio G., 9, 44298 Kaunas, Lithuania is the address.

Fargo Co.: With a cuisine that suits a variety of palates and a contemporary industrial style, Fargo Co. distinguishes out. It's a flexible place for different tastes, offering everything from specialized coffees to fresh juices and mouthwatering pastries. Maironio G., 11, 44298 Kaunas, Lithuania is the address.

Every one of these popular hangouts and cafés in Kaunas adds a unique touch to the city's coffee scene. Whether you're looking for a modern urban vibe, feline company, or riverside peace, these cafés in Lithuania encourage you to stay awhile, make friends with the people, and make wonderful memories.

CHAPTER 3

Must-see Sights

Kaunas Castle

Salutations, connoisseurs of history! Time travel to the center of Kaunas, where the recognizable Kaunas Castle towers over the banks of the Nemunas River. Explore this medieval fortress's illustrious heritage as a representation of tenacity and endurance.

History and Architecture: Built in the fourteenth century, Kaunas Castle is located at Maironio g., 7, 44298 Kaunas, Lithuania. It was originally built of wood, but to withstand the test of time, it was later reconstructed in stone. The castle saw conflicts, changes, and even a period when it was home to nobles over the ages.

Explore the castle grounds, which are encircled by towers and protective walls that evoke memories of medieval Lithuania. The Donjon, the fortress's main tower, gives visitors sweeping views of the city and the river and sheds light on the fortress's strategic significance.

Exploration and Exhibitions: Upon entering the castle, you will see a fascinating display detailing the history of Kaunas Castle. Exhibits feature artifacts and archeological discoveries that tell the story of the castle's development and the lives of its occupants.

The castle provides tourists with an immersive experience by hosting a variety of activities, such as cultural festivals and medieval reenactments. Feel like you've been transported back in time to observe expert craftspeople in action or take part in medieval-themed events inside the castle walls.

Practical Information: Kaunas Castle is open to visitors all year round. The entrance price is roughly four euros, and the opening hours are typically from 10 am to 6 pm. For information on any special events or temporary closures, see the official website or the local listings.

Pazaislis Monastery

Ah, the tranquil Pazaislis Monastery, a hidden treasure tucked away in Kaunas' verdant surroundings. Come along with me as we tour Pazaislis, a serene hideaway for individuals in need of serenity and a masterwork of Baroque architecture.

Spiritual Legacy: Spiritual Heritage is situated at T. Pazaislis Monastery, located at Masiulio G., 31, 44294 Kaunas, Lithuania, and has a long and illustrious history that dates back to the 17th century. The Order of the Camaldolese nuns found refuge in the monastery, which was founded by Maria Kazimiera, Queen of Poland, Grand Duchess of Lithuania, Duchess of Courland, and Semigallia.

Admire the exterior's Baroque splendor. Once inside, the exquisite stucco work, elaborate chapels, and breathtaking murals will wow you. The magnificent Baroque style is demonstrated by the Monastery Church, which is devoted to the Assumption of the Virgin Mary.

Architectural Magnificence: Pazaislis is a masterwork of architecture, not only a monastery. In addition to the church, the complex includes lovely gardens, a tower, and a convent.

An aura of awe is created by the Baroque-style components, which include the exquisitely constructed ceiling and the elaborate altar.

With its expansive views of the surrounding landscape, the tower beckons you to ascend its steps and experience the peace of the monastery grounds. The calm gardens are the ideal place to reflect and unwind thanks to their geometric designs and abundant vegetation.

Events and Concerts: Pazaislis Monastery has developed into a center of culture in addition to its spiritual importance. The monastery holds several events, such as art exhibits and concerts of classical music. The church's acoustics make it a popular location for performers, bringing in crowds from all over.

See what performances or activities are scheduled while you're there, and take in the harmonic fusion of cultural enrichment within the monastery's hallowed walls.

Useful Information: Every day, people are welcome to visit Pazaislis Monastery. Usually, the store is open from 10 a.m. to 6 p.m. There is an approximate 4 Euro admission price; guided tours and special events may incur additional costs. It's best to consult local sources or the official website for the most up-to-date details on events and operating hours.

Liberty Avenue

Welcome to Liberty Avenue, Kaunas's vibrant center! This lively street, which connects the Old Town and the New Town, is alive with activity, business, and Kaunas spirit. Come along with me as we explore the charms and tales this famous avenue has to offer.

A Walk Through Time: Kaunas's Liberty Avenue, also known as Laisvės alėja, is more than just a roadway; it serves as a historical chronicle. The avenue first appeared in the years between the wars, when the independent Republic of Lithuania was established. It still serves as a testament to the tenacity of the city and the rapid development of its urban environment.

In Maironio g., 9, 44298 Kaunas, Lithuania, you can begin your adventure with the statue of Maironis, a well-known poet from Lithuania. This is the start of Liberty Avenue, which takes you on an enthralling voyage through culture and history.

Shopping and Dining: Liberty Avenue is lined with a colorful assortment of stores, boutiques, and cafes. The avenue is a shoppers' haven, with everything from worldwide brands to local artists showing off their wares. Take a moment to peruse the quaint bookstores, chic boutiques, and distinctive gift shops that line the avenue.
With a wide variety of cafes and eateries, the Boulevard is also a culinary treat. Liberty Avenue offers something for every palate, be it international cuisine, pleasant

coffee breaks, or traditional Lithuanian meals.

Cultural Landmarks: Liberty Avenue's charm is enhanced by the presence of numerous cultural landmarks. The Great War Museum in Vytautas is located at K. Located in Donelaičio g., 64, 44248 Kaunas, Lithuania, it honors the country's military heritage. The Maironis Lithuanian Literature Museum honors the literary heritage of the country and is situated at Rotušės a., 13, 44298 Kaunas, Lithuania. Keep an eye out for the interesting sculptures and public artworks that line the Boulevard as you proceed. These artistic expressions give your trip down Liberty Avenue a dash of originality.

Events & Celebrations: Liberty Avenue serves as a vibrant stage for a variety of events and celebrations, not just a dull roadway. The avenue is home to a wide range of events all year long, including markets, outdoor concerts, parades, and cultural festivities. Look for any forthcoming celebrations during your visit on the calendars of local events.

Useful Information: Liberty Avenue extends a warm invitation to guests at any time. Throughout their designated business hours, the stores and cafes are open. It is advisable to check in advance for any special events or closures as the museums along the route may have unique opening hours and entry rates.

Discover the layers of spirituality, urban energy, and history that make up this extraordinary Lithuanian city as you walk down Liberty Avenue, Kaunas Castle, and Pazaislis Monastery. Kaunas calls with stories waiting to be found, whether you're enthralled by Baroque wonders, mesmerized by medieval strongholds, or engrossed in the bustling pulse of a city boulevard.

Vytautas the Great War Museum

Salutations, connoisseurs of history! Today, we visit the Vytautas the Great War Museum, a military history archive tucked away along lively Liberty Avenue in K, where we go on a tour through the remnants of wartime Lithuania. 64, 44248 Kaunas, Lithuania is Donelaičio G.

Historical Significance: The Vytautas the Great War Museum was established in 1921 and is a monument to Lithuania's fortitude in the face of war.

The museum, which bears the name of Grand Duke Vytautas, a significant character in Lithuanian history, documents Lithuania's military history, spanning from medieval conflicts to independence movements.

Exhibitions & Collections: The museum greets you with a huge array of relics, armaments, and records that portray Lithuania's military history as soon as you walk in. Explore the exhibit halls, where artifacts depict the intricacies of medieval combat, the struggles for freedom, and the difficulties encountered in both World Wars. The outstanding collection of weapons, which displays weapons used by Lithuanian warriors throughout history, is one of the attractions. Every item, from 20th-century guns to ancient swords, narrates the tale of the nation's changing military might.

Tribute to Independence: The museum honors the nation of Lithuania's valiant struggle for freedom. Examine the displays honoring the early 20th century's battles, such as the 1918–1920 War of Independence. Memorabilia from the liberation fighters, including pictures and documents, provide a moving look into this important period in Lithuanian history.

Memorials & Outdoor Displays: Head outside to the areas where somber war memorials are surrounded by lush vegetation. With its collection of historical military vehicles, Tank Square offers a visual tour of Lithuania's military development. The atmosphere serves as a moving reminder of those who gave their lives in defense of the country.

Useful Information: Throughout the week, visitors are welcome to the Vytautas the Great War Museum. The entrance price is roughly 4 Euros, and the regular opening hours are 10 am to 6 pm. If there are any special exhibitions, events, or adjustments to the usual timetable, be sure to check the museum's website.

Maironis Lithuanian Literature Museum

Come with me to the Maironis Lithuanian Literature Museum, where I will take you on a cultural tour exploring the pages of Lithuania's literary heritage. Located in Rotušės a., 13, 44298 Kaunas, Lithuania, right in the center of Liberty Avenue, this museum honors the writers who have influenced the literary landscape of the country.

Paying tribute to Maironis: Maironis is a well-regarded poet in Lithuania, and the museum bears his name. The calm atmosphere of the museum welcomes you as you go in and honors Maironis's contributions to Lithuanian literature. His life, his creations, and the influence of his poetry on culture are all exquisitely displayed in the museum's rooms.

Exhibitions & Manuscripts: Stroll around the exhibition areas to see rare books, manuscripts, and personal items belonging to well-known Lithuanian authors unfolding in front of you. With its vast collection of literary objects, the museum offers valuable insights into the creative processes of well-known writers.

Special exhibitions provide visitors with a dynamic experience every time they visit, with a focus on particular periods, subjects, or literary movements. The museum embodies Lithuanian writing culture via both modern and traditional Lithuanian literature.

Interactive Areas and Events: Interact with books in areas intended to stimulate creativity. The museum supports a vibrant literary community by holding events, book launches, and readings regularly. If there are any events scheduled during your stay, make sure to check the schedule. You might be able to attend a literary event or engage with local authors.

Garden of Literature: Enter this outdoor haven where landscape sculptures honoring well-known Lithuanian authors are situated. In the center of Kaunas, this serene area promotes introspection and contemplation while offering a distinctive fusion of culture and environment.

Practical Information: 10 a.m. to 6 p.m. is when guests can visit the Maironis Lithuanian Literature Museum. Seniors and students can receive reductions on the about 4 Euro admission price. For information on any upcoming events, special exhibitions, or adjustments to the usual timetable, check out the museum's website.

You are immersing yourself in Lithuania's essence as you explore the Maironis Lithuanian Literature Museum and the Vytautas the Great War Museum, not just learning about literature and history. These museums serve as stewards of the nation's history, providing an engrossing trip through the achievements, difficulties, and cultural diversity that characterize this exceptional country on the Baltic Sea.

CHAPTER 4

Immersing in Culture

Kaunas Old Town

Greetings from Kaunas's Old Town, the lovely center of the city! With its medieval elegance, cobblestone streets, and rich history, this neighborhood encourages you to travel back in time and experience the spirit of Lithuania's cultural legacy.

Historic Highlights: Kaunas Old Town is a fascinating tapestry of architectural gems, tucked away on the banks of the Nemunas

River. Set out on your adventure at Town Hall Square, the busy center where the past and current meet.

The magnificent Gothic Town Hall itself is a representation of community pride.

Explore the charming, small lanes with their vibrant facades to find hidden treasures like the Kaunas Castle, located at Maironio g., 7, 44298 Kaunas, Lithuania. Tales of heroic ancestry and valiant wars are murmured from this proudly perched medieval stronghold on the riverbank. Climb the Donjon Tower to see sweeping views of the city.

Sacred Sanctuaries: Numerous sacred sanctuaries around the Old Town attest to centuries of religious belief. Situated at Maironio g., 9, 44298 Kaunas, Lithuania, St. George the Martyr Church is a calm sanctuary featuring elaborate murals and a peaceful patio.

Proceed to the Kaunas Cathedral Basilica, an outstanding 15th-century building, to complete your journey. Admire its Baroque splendor and venture inside the crypt that holds the relics of Grand Dukes and other notable historical personalities.

Cozy cafés and Craft Shops: Stop for a leisurely break at one of the numerous quaint cafés in Old Town as you stroll through the area. Enjoy a delicious treat or a cup of Lithuanian coffee while you take in the quaint setting. The Old Town is a great place to find one-of-a-kind keepsakes because it is lined with artisanal stores selling handcrafted goods and souvenirs.

Useful Information: Kaunas Old Town is a charming maze that just begs to be discovered. Explore at your speed, take in the atmosphere of the Middle Ages, and find undiscovered treasures everywhere you turn. Because the majority of the sights are conveniently located on foot, you can fully immerse yourself in the rich history and culture of this ageless neighborhood.

While cafes and stores may have different hours, historically significant locations like Kaunas Castle and the cathedrals usually open from 10 am to 6 pm. It is advisable to check in advance for any special events or closures as certain places may charge an admission fee.

Let's now move on to another aspect of Kaunas's cultural scene: its thriving museums and art galleries.

Art Galleries and Museums

Take a cultural tour of six vibrant museums and art galleries in Kaunas that highlight the city's artistic development and creative energy.

M. K. Čiurlionis National Art Museum: M. K. The Čiurlionis National Art Museum honors the visionary artist and composer Mikalojus Konstantinas Čiurlionis and is situated at V. Putvinskio g., 55, 44211 Kaunas, Lithuania. A sizable collection of his artwork, musical works, and personal items are kept in the museum. Explore the realm of Čiurlionis's creative inventiveness and symbolism. The entrance price is around five euros, and the opening hours are usually from 11 am to 5 pm.

Devil's Museum: Located at Maironio g., 6, 44298 Kaunas, Lithuania, this eccentric delight features an intriguing collection of devil sculptures from all around the world. Discover the various ways that this mythological character has been interpreted and delight in the amusing ambiance. The museum charges an admission price of about three euros and is open from Wednesday through Sunday from 11 am to 5 pm.

Juozas Zikaras Sculpture Gallery: Explore the universe of Lithuanian sculptor Juozas Zikaras at the Juozas Zikaras Sculpture Gallery, which is situated at Maironio g., 6, 44298 Kaunas, Lithuania. Admire the sculptor's exquisite work and learn about his creative process. The gallery usually opens Wednesday through Sunday from 11 a.m. to 5 p.m. Admission is about two euros.

Kaunas Picture Gallery: The Kaunas Picture Gallery, located at 16 Donelaičio G., 44298 Kaunas, Lithuania, is a lively venue honoring Lithuanian modern art. Look into changing exhibitions including multimedia installations, sculptures, and paintings. The gallery's hours of operation change, so it's best to check ahead. There can be an admission charge, depending on the show.

Maironis Lithuanian Literature Museum: Rotušės a., 13, 44298 Kaunas, Lithuania is home to this literary sanctuary, as was previously mentioned. Explore manuscripts, learn about the literary heritage of Lithuanian authors, and take in the inspiring atmosphere of the Maironis Lithuanian Literature Museum. The museum is usually open from 10 a.m. to 6 p.m. and costs about 4 euros to enter.

Kaunas Photography Gallery: Kaunas Photography Gallery is a gallery that showcases the artistic talent of both local and foreign photographers. It is located in Vilijampolė, an eclectic district. For those who enjoy photography, Maironio g., 21, 44298 Kaunas, Lithuania, offers a visual feast. Depending on the show, opening hours may change, so it's best to check ahead. The cost of admission varies depending on the exhibition.

Useful Information: Culture vultures can enjoy a variety of experiences at Kaunas's museums and art galleries. It's best to check the websites or local listings of the individual venues for the most up-to-date information regarding opening hours, entrance costs, and exhibition schedules as these can change.

Take a cultural tour of Kaunas, where innovation, art, and history come together to create a dynamic tapestry that represents Lithuania's rich cultural past. Kaunas invites exploration, with tales waiting to be discovered, whether you choose to take in the modern artwork of regional artists or explore the Old Town's medieval splendor.

Folk Traditions and Festivals

Take a trip through the rich cultural fabric of Kaunas as we explore seven folk customs and celebrations that enliven the city with dancing, music, and a sense of togetherness.

Joninės (Rasos): On the shortest night of the year, which falls on or around June 23rd, celebrate the magical Joninės, also known as Rasos. Take part in the celebrations at the parks nearby, where bonfires light up the night sky, or beside the Nemunas River. Experience the enchantment of folk music, dancing, and customs as residents unite to celebrate the summer solstice.

Užgavėnės: Say goodbye to winter with Užgavėnės' colorful pre-Lenten carnival. This festive event, which takes place in late February or early March, is marked by masked processions, folk music, and the consumption of mouthwatering pancakes known as "blynai." Join the people in parks throughout Kaunas for a day filled with fun, silly costumes, and the spirit of renewal.

St. John's Day (Joninės): Celebrate St. John's Day (Joninės) on June 24th to celebrate the start of summer. Join the locals for a night of traditional music, bonfires, and wreath-making along the Nemunas River or in parks like Santakos Parkas. Take part in the festive mood as Lithuanians honor this important day that is entrenched in both pagan and Christian customs.

Kaunas Jazz Festival: Savor the rich melodies and pulsating beats of this yearly celebration of jazz that reverberates throughout the city. Although the locations of the festival may change, the Kaunas State Philharmonic Society, located at Maironio g., 25, 44298 Kaunas, Lithuania, is frequently the center of the festivities. See the festival calendar for jazz concerts by regional and worldwide performers, resulting in a pleasing fusion of musical styles and cultural expressions.

Pažaislis Music Festival: This event, which takes place at the Pažaislis Monastery at T, offers a taste of classical music. Masiulio G., 31, Kaunas, 44294, Lithuania. This Baroque masterwork serves as the backdrop for orchestral, chamber, and recital performances that are part of the festival. Indulge in the alluring atmosphere of Pažaislis, where architectural magnificence blends with the eternal beauty of music.

International Kaunas Film Festival: Happy viewing, lovers of movies! The city's several locations host the International

Kaunas Film Festival, which uncovers cinematic marvels. View the schedule of events for the festival to learn about talks, screenings, and chances to interact with filmmakers. Locations such as the Kaunas Cinema Center at Maironio g., 7, 44298 Kaunas, Lithuania, may serve as the festival's main hub. Explore the world of storytelling via this lens, where a variety of stories enthrall listeners.

Christmas in Kaunas: Experience the enchantment of Kaunas' Christmastime, when the Old Town is transformed into a wintry paradise. Discover the Town Hall Square Christmas Market, which is lit up with holiday lights and has booths selling baked goods and crafts. Enjoy the sounds of carol singers, warm up with mulled wine, and take in the festive mood. The holiday season is magical for both locals and visitors because of the spreading joyful spirit.

Exploring Restaurants and Markets

Set off on a gastronomic journey around Kaunas as we investigate regional fare and marketplaces that entice the senses with a variety of traditional flavors.

Bernelių Užeiga: Enjoy comfort food from Lithuania at this well-known restaurant, which is situated at Maironio g., 9, 44298 Kaunas, Lithuania. Savor traditional dishes such as kugelis, potato pudding, or cepelinai served with sour cream. For those looking for an authentic Lithuanian dining experience, it's a popular choice because of its cozy atmosphere and generous quantities.

Amandus: Located in Maironio g., 9, 44298 Kaunas, Lithuania, Amandus offers a fusion of European and Lithuanian cuisine. The menu features a delicious fusion of tastes with a contemporary take on classic meals. Savor a homey meal amid Old Town, where inventive cooking takes center stage.

Senoji Trobelė: Located at Maironio g., 9, 44298 Kaunas, Lithuania, this quaint restaurant invites you to immerse yourself in Lithuanian classics. The menu includes dishes such as šaltibarščiai (cold beet soup) and cepelinai, which showcase the region's rich culinary legacy. Your culinary adventure is made more authentic by the Old Town setting.

Kaunas Farmers' Market: Visit the lively Kaunas Farmers' Market at Maironio g., 3, 44298 Kaunas, Lithuania, where regional sellers offer handcrafted items, fresh food, and traditional treats.
Wander among the colorful stalls, chat with vendors, and savor local cheeses, smoked meats, and preserves. Every day the market is open, providing a vibrant setting for gastronomic discovery.

Žaliakalnis Market: Visit Taikos PR to enjoy the Žaliakalnis Market, located in the Žaliakalnis area. 84 Kaunas, 51132, Lithuania. This market offers a wide variety of goods, from fresh fruit to handcrafted crafts, and gives an insight into the everyday lives of the residents. Have discussions with sellers to find out more about Kaunas's culinary customs.

Kaunas Coffee Festival: This event is a must-attend for anyone who likes coffee. Coffee enthusiasts may anticipate a celebration of various coffee flavors, brewing methods, and creative presentations, even though the festival's locations may change. For workshops, tastings, and a chance to learn more about Kaunas's vibrant coffee culture, check out the festival schedule.

Kaunas Street Food Market: Enjoy a culinary journey at the Kaunas Street Food Market, where a variety of merchants assemble to present a wide selection of both local and foreign street food delicacies. For the most recent details, see your local event listings as the market's location may change. With a wide variety of savory and sweet options, the market serves a wide range of palates.

Holy Donut: Holy Donut, located at Maironio g., 9, 44298 Kaunas, Lithuania, is the place to satisfy your sweet tooth. This quaint bakery specializes in creatively twisted artisanal donuts. Savor tastes like matcha, pistachio, or traditional glazed, then wash it down with a good cup of coffee. The pleasurable experience of enjoying these delicious delicacies is enhanced by the warm ambiance.

Useful Information: Check local event calendars for festival dates, locations, and program details before visiting. While many activities are free, some—especially seminars or performances—may require tickets. Be prepared and enjoy the distinctive cultural experiences that every festival has to offer.

Operating hours for restaurants sometimes change, so it's best to check their websites or get in touch with them directly to find out the most recent details. Even though some restaurants could take credit cards, it's always a good idea to have extra cash on hand, especially when visiting new marketplaces.

Kaunas welcomes you to experience its lively festivals, where customs come to life, and its varied food scene, where tastes narrate tales of a rich past. Every time you spend in Kaunas reveals a new chapter in the city's cultural and culinary story, whether you're dancing at Joninės, perusing the Kaunas Farmers' Market, or enjoying the inventiveness of the region's chefs.

Kaunas Local Cuisine

Savor the delicious flavors of Kaunas as we take a look at seven meals that are a must-try and highlight the diverse range of Lithuanian cuisine.

Cepelinai: Get ready to enjoy the traditional cepelinai, which are potato dumplings filled with either minced meat, curd, or mushrooms. A true Lithuanian staple, these zeppelin-shaped delicacies are topped with bacon pieces and sour cream, creating a savory symphony. For a genuine experience, enjoy this filling dish at Bernelių Užeiga, which is situated at Maironio g., 9, 44298 Kaunas, Lithuania.

Šaltibarščiai (Cold Beet Soup): This cool beet soup is a great way to stay cool on hot days. Beets, cucumbers, hard-boiled eggs, and dill are combined with kefir or buttermilk to create this bright pink combination. The outcome is a delicious and nutritious soup that is chilled and has a hint of acidity. This cool dish is served at several neighborhood cafes and restaurants in Kaunas.

Kugelis: Kugelis is a Lithuanian potato pudding that can satisfy your demands for comfort food. Baked to golden perfection, grated potatoes are combined with eggs, onions, and bacon. The end product is a hearty, slightly crunchy meal that's usually served with applesauce or sour cream. At Senoji Trobelė, located at Maironio g., 9, 44298 Kaunas, Lithuania, savor this classic treat.

Potato Pancakes, or Bulviniai Blynai: Indulge in Lithuanian potato pancakes that are just the right amount of crunchy and fluffy. These flavorful pancakes, frequently paired with sour cream or applesauce, are a popular comfort dish. Savor this delicious dish in several cafés and restaurants in

Kaunas, each putting their own special spin on this traditional dish.

Skilandis: Experience the unique flavor of Lithuanian smoked sausage, known for its smokey deliciousness. Skilandis is a delectably powerful dish made from minced meat, garlic, and a combination of spices that is then air-dried and cold-smoked. You can find this regional specialty at markets and specialized stores such as the Kaunas Farmers' Market, located at Maironio g., 3, 44298 Kaunas, Lithuania.

Kibinai: Savory pastries stuffed with cheese, meat, or veggies are a great way to start a gastronomic journey. The Karaim people brought these flaky treats to Lithuanian cuisine.
Sample several kibinai varieties at neighborhood bakeries and cafes where creativity and tradition collide, like Holy Donut at Maironio g., 9, 44298 Kaunas, Lithuania.

Suktinukai: Savor the tastes of these mouthwatering and aesthetically pleasing wrapped pork pancakes. Rolls with a filling of cheese, mushrooms, or vegetables are made from thin slices of meat, usually chicken or pork. Then these tasty morsels are perfectly pan-fried. Savor suktinukai in several Kaunas eateries, where Lithuanian culinary creativity is on display.

Useful Information: Make sure to verify the restaurant and cafe hours when sampling the local fare in Kaunas. A dash of surprise might be added to your gastronomic adventure with select establishments serving distinctive dishes as daily specials or during particular seasons.

Even while most places accept cards, it's still a good idea to carry extra cash, particularly when going to smaller restaurants or local markets. To guarantee a fun and secure dining experience, also ask about any dietary requirements or allergies when sampling new foods.

Savor the genuine flavors of Lithuanian cuisine at Kaunas, where every dish narrates a tale of creativity, history, and the lively spirit of this extraordinary city. Every morsel reveals a new chapter in Kaunas's culinary story, whether you're savoring traditional dishes like cepelinai or trying out contemporary takes on regional favorites.

CHAPTER 5

Adventures in Nature

Nemunas Loops Regional Park

Welcome to Nemunas Loops Regional Park, a hidden jewel in the center of Lithuania, for those who enjoy the great outdoors. Join us as we go through this stunning area, which offers peace, biodiversity, and a close-up encounter with the natural world.

Location: Nemunas Loops Regional Park is a vast area that contains both natural reserves and cultural heritage sites. It spans along the Nemunas River's meandering bends. The park's headquarters are located at 14 Pravieniškių g., 14195 Kaunas, Lithuania.

Magnificent Sceneries: Nemunas Loops Regional Park is a natural wonderland with a wide variety of sceneries. Discover verdant woodlands, winding riverbanks, and picturesque vantage spots that reveal the Nemunas River's captivating loops. The landscape of the park provides an excellent backdrop for outdoor pursuits, such as serene treks and birdwatching amid the many wildlife that calls this area home.

Must-Visit Points:

- Raudondvaris Castle: Start your adventure at this park's historic treasure, Raudondvaris Castle. This Renaissance-style castle offers a fascinating look into Lithuania's illustrious past and is situated at Vytauto g., 2, Raudondvaris, Kaunas District Municipality, Lithuania. It is surrounded by a sizable park. To make the most of your stay, look into events and guided tours.
- Panemunė Castle: Located in Pilviškių k., 2, Naujoji Akmenė Municipality, Lithuania, is another noteworthy landmark. Perched boldly on the banks of the Nemunas River, this ancient fortification provides an intriguing window into Lithuania's history. Take in the gorgeous views of

the river loops as you stroll around the castle grounds.

Outdoor Activities: With a wide range of offerings, Nemunas Loops Regional Park is a haven for outdoor enthusiasts. You are welcome to stroll along the hiking trails, which are located close to Raudondvaris Castle, to discover the park's scenic surroundings. Cyclists can ride on designated routes and enjoy the tranquil surroundings.

Practical Information: Due to the park's year-round opening, visitors may observe the varying seasons as well as the wide variety of plants and animals. While much of Nemunas Loops Regional Park is free to enter, some locations, like Raudondvaris Castle, may charge a separate admission fee. For information on any guided tours, special events, or alterations to the regular schedule, visit the park's website.

Let's now turn our attention to the calm Kaunas Reservoir, whose placid waters entice us.

Kaunas Reservoir

Admire the tranquility of Kaunas Reservoir, a sizable watery haven that skillfully combines leisure options with the splendor of nature. Come along with me as we discover the serene beaches, aquatic pursuits, and picturesque charm that render the reservoir an oasis for leisure and exploration.

Location: Across the Nemunas River, Kaunas Reservoir, also called Kauno Marios, provides a tranquil haven from the busy city life. Nemuno g., 4, 44220 Kaunas, Lithuania is the starting point for your exploration of the reservoir's shoreline, which is easily accessible.

Natural Beauty: The 60-kilometer-long Kaunas Reservoir is a breathtaking freshwater reservoir encircled by undulating hills and luxuriant vegetation. The reservoir's banks are lined with gorgeous scenery, which makes it a great place for leisurely walks, picnics, or just taking in the tranquil surroundings.

Recreational Activities:

- Boating and Sailing: Rent a boat or go sailing to enjoy the tranquil seas. The vastness of the reservoir makes for tranquil boating adventures and provides a special viewpoint of the surrounding scenic beauties.
- Fishing: Take up the ancient pastime of fishing by dipping a line into the calm waters. The reservoir is a favorite location for fishermen because it is home to a variety of fish species. Before you cast your line, find out what the local laws are and, if required, get permits.
- Cycling and Hiking: Trails for cycling and hiking encircle the reservoir's shoreline, offering an opportunity to

take in the picturesque surroundings. The reservoir's routes are suitable for all skill levels of outdoor lovers, whether your preference is a leisurely bike ride or a serene stroll.

Important Points

- Rumšiškės: Visit the Open-Air Museum of Lithuania in the adjacent town of Rumšiškės. The museum offers an engrossing trip through Lithuania's past by showcasing traditional architecture and cultural heritage.
- Pažaislis Monastery: Enjoy the architectural magnificence of Pažaislis Monastery, which is situated at T. Masiulio G., 31, Kaunas, 44294, Lithuania. This Baroque masterpiece is tucked away next to the reservoir and is surrounded by tranquil gardens, beautifully fusing nature and culture.

Useful Information: Kaunas Reservoir is open to visitors all year round, with a distinct appeal for each season. Although there isn't a set price to enter the reservoir, there could be fees for some activities like boat rentals or guided tours. For more details on recreational services and amenities, visit the reservoir's website or speak with nearby suppliers.

Allow the serenity of the water and the breathtaking scenery around you to melt away the cares of daily life as you explore the shores of Kaunas Reservoir. The reservoir provides a calm haven close to Kaunas's lively atmosphere, whether you're looking for outdoor activities or just a quiet getaway.

Zaliakalnis Funicular Railway

Reach new heights on the Zaliakalnis Funicular Railway, a famous piece of infrastructure that not only links two Kaunas neighborhoods but also provides amazing views of the entire city. Come along with me for a magical ride on this antique funicular, where comfort and nostalgia collide.

Location: Maironio g., 10, 44298 Kaunas, Lithuania, and Vytauto pr., 16, 44298 Kaunas, Lithuania, are the destinations of the Zaliakalnis Funicular Railway. This funicular, which is conveniently located close to the city center, offers a picturesque connection between the lower and upper regions of Kaunas.

Historical Charm: Travel back in time when you ride the Zaliakalnis Funicular, a 1931-era relic from Kaunas' past. The funicular offers a unique experience reminiscent of a bygone period and still has its lovely wooden coaches. Take in expansive views of the Neris River and the adjacent neighborhoods as you move up or down the slope.

Scenic Delights: Travelers who ride the Zaliakalnis Funicular are treated to charming views of Kaunas, making for an unforgettable experience that blends practicality with aesthetic pleasure. Admire the architectural diversity that characterizes Kaunas and take in the cityscape from higher viewpoints.

Practical Information: Convenient transit between Kaunas's lower and upper regions is offered by the Zaliakalnis Funicular, which is open during regular business hours. Even if the rate is usually reasonable, it's a good idea to inquire about any changes to ticket costs, timetables for operations, and maintenance. For tourists and locals alike, the funicular is a must-experience since it provides a charming and effective means of getting around the city.

Outdoor Activities and Hiking Trails

Discover the beautiful outdoors in Kaunas with an abundance of hiking routes and outdoor activities that appeal to both nature enthusiasts and thrill seekers. Come along with me as we explore the varied scenery and outdoor activities that make Kaunas a sanctuary for anyone who loves the outdoors and open spaces.

Lush Greenery at Pazaislis Park: Pazaislis Park, at T, is a great place to start your outdoor excursion. Masiulio G., 31, Kaunas, 44294, Lithuania. This large park offers a unique combination of rich cultural diversity and scenic beauty. Explore pathways surrounded by trees, uncover sculpture-adorned nooks, and find peace along the Kaunas Reservoir's edge.

Hiking Trails Near Zaliakalnis Hill: The Zaliakalnis Funicular makes it simple to trek in the vicinity of Zaliakalnis Hill. Discover the system of trails that offer breathtaking views of the city while winding through verdant woodlands. Trekkers can select routes based on their interests, ranging from easy strolls to strenuous climbs.

Adventures in Kaunas Botanical Garden: Visit the Kaunas Botanical Garden, located at Maironio g., 24, 44298 Kaunas, Lithuania, to discover the beauties of nature.
This verdant haven features a variety of plant life, calm ponds, and themed gardens. Trace well-kept pathways, take in the crisp air filled with blooming floral scents, and enjoy a tranquil escape right in the middle of the city.

Nemunas Loops Regional Park - Outdoor Haven: Go back to Nemunas

Loops Regional Park for a more comprehensive outdoor experience. Take part in a variety of outdoor pursuits, such as cycling on defined routes or birdwatching. The park is a refuge for people looking to get back in touch with nature because of its varied landscapes, which provide chances for both adventure and leisure.

Useful Information: Take the season and weather into account when enjoying outdoor activities in Kaunas. The Kaunas Botanical Garden, Zaliakalnis Hill, and Pazaislis Park are just a few examples of locations that could have different admission prices and hours. For the most recent details on the facilities, guided tours, and any special events, visit the corresponding websites or get in touch with the locations directly.

Kaunas welcomes you to appreciate the beauty of outdoor experiences, whether you're taking in the views of the city from the top of the Zaliakalnis Funicular or discovering the natural beauties of Pazaislis Park and surrounding areas. A revitalizing getaway in the center of Lithuania's energetic capital is promised by the hiking paths, green areas, and picturesque overlooks.

CHAPTER 6

Thrilling Experiences

Hot Air Balloon Rides

Take a Hot Air Balloon Ride to broaden your view of Kaunas and go on a fantastical journey. Come fly with me and take in the splendor of the city from an amazing vantage point.

Location: Depending on the weather, Kaunas' hot air balloon ride launch place frequently changes. Businesses such as "Ballooning.lt" frequently conduct flights; they may take off from Maironio g., 3, 44298 Kaunas, Lithuania, or other specified sites. It's best to inquire with the particular business for the most recent details regarding launch locations.

Aerial Panorama: As the hot air balloon gently ascends above the ground, get ready for a breathtaking experience. As you soar over Kaunas, take in the monuments, architectural marvels, and scenic surroundings. Beneath you, the panoramic views weave a captivating tapestry of the Old Town, the Nemunas River, and the surrounding flora.

Sunrise and Sunset Flights: If possible, plan your hot air balloon ride for either the peaceful hours of the sunset or the early morning. The sun is shining warmly over Kaunas during these hours, adding to the allure of the surrounding scenery and creating a mystical ambiance. Capture the sky's shifting hues as well as the city below as it wakes up or closes.

Useful Information: To ensure a fun and safe experience, hot air balloon rides are usually arranged according to the weather. Businesses such as "Ballooning.lt" offer various packages, which frequently include the balloon ride, pre-flight briefings, and a post-flight celebration. For reservations and detailed information, it is best to verify with the company as prices can vary.

A safe flight is guaranteed by certified pilots, who place a high premium on safety.

Individuals, couples, or small groups can enjoy balloon rides, which provide a peaceful and personal experience far above Kaunas.

Kayaking on Nemunas River

Take a kayaking trip on the Nemunas River to fully experience the peace of the natural world. Come paddle with me as we discover hidden coves, take in breathtaking scenery, and enjoy the calming sound of the river.

Kayak Rental Locations: Start your kayak adventure at one of the places along the Nemunas River that offer kayaks. Businesses such as "Nemuno Turas" provide guided tours and kayak rentals. They are available from Vytauto PR. 37, 44352 Lithuania Kaunas. For information on availability and operation hours, contact the rental businesses.

Exploration of a Calm River: Immerse yourself in the peace of the Nemunas River by launching your kayak into its mild currents. Paddle at your speed, letting the river's steady flow lead you past verdant meadows and lovely vistas. For novices and experts alike, the Nemunas River provides a tranquil setting for kayaking.

Kaunas Reservoir Connection: If you're looking for a longer kayak trip, you might want to check out the route that connects the Kaunas Reservoir to the Nemunas River. From the waterway, you can see Kaunas from a different angle. You can see a variety of bird species, rich greenery, and a rare riverbank village.

Riverbank Relaxation and Picnic Areas: Take breaks from your kayaking adventure at these beautiful locations along the riverbanks. Bring a picnic and savor a meal by the river while taking in the peace of the natural world. There are designated rest areas and riverfront parks in some places, which make it the ideal place to enjoy the landscape, unwind, and cherish the moment.

Useful Information: Depending on one's tastes, kayaking on the Nemunas River is a flexible activity.

Rental firms such as "Nemuno Turas" frequently provide both single and tandem kayaks, hence facilitating accessibility for singles or couples. Based on the length of the rental and the services offered, prices may change.

Kayaking usually includes safety precautions such as life jackets and basic instructions. There can also be guided excursions offered for individuals who would rather explore in a more regimented manner. For exact information, age limitations, and whether reservations are necessary, especially during busy times of the year, get in touch with the rental provider.

The Nemunas River kayaking experience provides a tranquil way to disconnect from the outside world, regardless of one's level of skill. It's a fun activity for people who want to experience Kaunas's natural beauty because of the calm current, beautiful surroundings, and flexibility to go at your speed.

Nightlife in Kaunas

Kaunas comes alive at night with a thriving nightlife that suits a wide range of interests and inclinations when the sun sets. Come along as we discover Kaunas' vibrant nightlife, from bustling bars to popular cultural destinations.

Bar-Hopping on Maironio Street: Maironio Street is a center of vibrant bars and pubs where you may start your nighttime exploration. There is something for everyone, from chic cocktail bars to small, locally-owned businesses. Take a look at the inventive cocktail menu at "M. Petras ir ko," which is located nearby at Maironio g., 7, 44298 Kaunas, Lithuania, or enjoy a craft beer at "Bambalyne," which is located at Maironio g., 9, 44298 Kaunas, Lithuania.

Live Music at Lemmy: Lemmy Bar, located at Maironio g., 9, 44298 Kaunas, Lithuania, is a must-visit for music lovers. Live events at this location include acoustic acts and indie bands. Experience the local music scene to the fullest while lounging in Lemmy's cozy surroundings.

Cultural Evenings at Kaunas State Drama Theatre: Located at Maironio g., 13, 44298 Kaunas, Lithuania, this theater offers a vibrant nightlife. Look at the theater's calendar for evening shows, which include both modern and historic plays. The ancient atmosphere of the theater elevates your cultural experience.

Dancing at Apoteka Club: Apoteka Club, located at Maironio g., 9, 44298 Kaunas, Lithuania, is a well-liked hangout for people looking to dance the night away. A variety of musical genres are played at this lively club, creating a lively environment. Come enjoy an evening of energetic music and dancing with both locals and guests.

Late-Night Snacks at Lokys: End the evening with a trip to Lokys, a quaint restaurant with a distinctive medieval ambiance located at Stikliu g., 8, 01131 Vilnius, Lithuania. Even though Lokys is in Vilnius, it's still worthwhile to note for those who prefer to stay up late and are in the capital after spending the previous evening in Kaunas. Savor substantial Lithuanian food, such as traditional meals and game meats.

Useful Information: Kaunas's nightlife scene usually begins in the late evening and lasts until the wee hours of the morning. Even while a lot of clubs and pubs take credit cards, it's still a good idea to have some cash on hand—especially for smaller businesses. For details on special events, theme evenings, or any admittance requirements, visit the websites or social media pages of the individual locations.

Let's now discuss another facet of Kaunas's allure: its distinctive shopping opportunities and the ideal mementos to take home.

Unique Shopping and Souvenirs

Set out on a shopping expedition in Kaunas, where charming markets and stores provide an abundance of unusual discoveries and regionally made mementos. Come along with me as we stroll through the quaint streets and find the ideal souvenirs to bring back home.

Crafty Finds at Maironio Street: Stroll down Maironio Street to see galleries and boutiques that highlight the creations of regional artists. Discover "Vardo Reiksme " in Maironio g., 9, 44298 Kaunas, Lithuania, for one-of-a-kind accessories, handcrafted jewelry, and creative pieces that embody Kaunas's inventive spirit.

Artistic Souvenirs at Kaunas Artists' House: Visit the Kaunas Artists' House, located at V. Putvinskio g., 56, 44298 Kaunas, Lithuania, to purchase artistic souvenirs. It is a cultural center with galleries, studios, and a store selling artwork created by regional artists. Find unique prints, paintings, ceramics, and other creative mementos that capture the essence of Kaunas' thriving arts culture.

Kaunas' Symbols at Kaunas Castle Gift Shop: Discover treasures at the Kaunas Castle Gift Shop, which is situated at Pilies g., 17, 44298 Kaunas, Lithuania. Explore "Kaunas' Symbols." This store, which is close to the ancient Kaunas Castle, sells a variety of mementos emblazoned with local icons. Choose from textiles and keychains to discover the ideal keepsake to remember your visit.

Unique Finds at Akropolis Shopping Mall: Visit the Akropolis Shopping Mall in Karaliaus Mindaugo pr., 49, 44333 Kaunas, Lithuania, for a more thorough shopping experience.
This mall offers a wide variety of merchandise and is home to both local and international retailers. For a comprehensive shopping experience, visit distinctive Lithuanian designer stores or look for well-known international brands.

Kaunas Market for Culinary Delights: Visit the Kaunas Market for Culinary Delights, located at Maironio g., 6, 44298 Kaunas, Lithuania, to sate your palate. A wide selection of regional food, handcrafted goods, and traditional Lithuanian delights are available at this lively market. Get some honey, specialty cheeses, or unusual condiments as tasty mementos.

Practical Information: Be aware that smaller stores may have different hours of operation when you explore Kaunas's shopping scene. Larger shopping centers often have regular business hours, while markets like the Kaunas Market are typically open every day. Souvenir prices can differ, so check out a few different stores to discover the ideal mix of value and cost.

Kaunas offers distinctive shopping experiences and souvenirs that allow you to bring a little piece of its beauty home with you. Every discovery you make, whether it's for handcrafted jewelry, artwork, or delicious food, reveals something new about Kaunas's vibrant creativity and rich cultural past.

CHAPTER 7

Practical Tips

Currency and Banking

Welcome to Kaunas, where a seamless and pleasurable visit is guaranteed with an awareness of the local currency and financial system. Let's start with the necessities, which include the official currency and practical banking procedures.

Official Currency: The Euro (€) is the official currency of Lithuania, which includes Kaunas. During your visit, make sure all of your financial transactions and budgeting are in euros.

Currency Exchange: Trustworthy locations such as banks, currency exchange offices, or ATMs are the best places to exchange currencies. Currency exchange services are available in the city center at places like SEB Bank, which is located at Maironio g., 25, 44298 Kaunas,

Lithuania. These businesses usually provide competitive rates, and it's easy to get cash out of them with the abundance of ATMs.

Payment methods: Hotels, restaurants, and larger establishments in Kaunas accept a variety of major credit and debit cards. But it's a good idea to have some cash on hand, particularly if you plan to explore smaller businesses, local markets, or take a taxi.

Hours of Operation: Banks in Kaunas are usually open from 9 AM to 5 PM, Monday through Friday. Remember that smaller branches or banks could operate on somewhat different schedules. On the other hand, cash is always available with ATMs.

Basics of Language: Knowing the basics of the local language will improve your interactions with the people you meet while exploring Kaunas. Although more and more people speak English, building connections might be facilitated by knowing a little bit of Lithuanian.

Common Phrases:
- Hello - Labas
- Thank you - Ačiū
- Please - Prašau
- Excuse me - Atsiprašau
- Goodbye - Viso gero

English Proficiency: Although many people in the area, particularly in the cities, speak English well, picking up a few simple Lithuanian words will be welcomed and frequently result in smiles. English is widely spoken in tourist-heavy locations, which facilitates smooth conversation.

Signage and Information: Materials in English and other languages are available in tourist information centers, like the one located at Maironio g., 25, 44298 Kaunas, Lithuania. English-language signage is also present in public transit and important attractions, making navigation simple.

Emergency Numbers: In Lithuania, 112 is the emergency number to call in case you need help. The majority of operators can connect you to the right assistance and speak English.

Safety and Health Tips

In Kaunas, ensuring your safety and well-being is our first concern. Let's discuss health-related facts and safety measures to ensure a worry-free visit.

Emergency Services: Dial 112 in the event of an emergency, including the need for police or medical assistance. Operators can direct you and put you in touch with the appropriate services. clinics such as Kaunas Clinics, which are situated at Eivenig. 2, 50161 Kaunas, Lithuania, provides workers who speak English for medical care.

Crime and Personal Safety: Kaunas is a fairly safe city, although you should always exercise caution when in any urban area. Be cautious with valuables, stay away from dimly lit streets at night, and keep an eye on your possessions in crowded areas. Even though occurrences are uncommon, having awareness increases security.

Health Warnings: The healthcare system in Lithuania is highly developed. Make sure your travel insurance is comprehensive and includes medical coverage. Kaunas maintain strict hygienic regulations, therefore the tap water is safe to drink. For over-the-counter drugs and medical supplies, pharmacies like Euroapotheca in Maironio g., 21, 44298 Kaunas, Lithuania, are easily accessible.

Health Services and vaccines: Find out if any vaccines are advised before visiting Kaunas. Pharmacies offer a variety of drugs, and health services are conveniently available. Before your vacation, discuss any specific health concerns you may have with your healthcare professional.

Local Customs: Having respect for customs from the area helps make things enjoyable. Politeness and a measured approach to public conduct are valued by Lithuanians. When visiting someone's home, it is traditional to take off your shoes, and being modest is usually favorably welcomed.

Practical Considerations: Kaunas's bus and trolleybus public transit systems are kept up nicely. When utilizing public transportation, especially during rush hours, keep a watch on your possessions. Although they are generally accessible and thought to be safe, taxis should only be used by reliable businesses.

In conclusion, Kaunas extends a confident invitation for you to discover its dynamic city life and rich cultural legacy. Get acquainted with the local currency, learn a few basic Lithuanian words, and put your health and safety first. Whether exploring the city center or taking part in cultural events, these useful suggestions guarantee an enjoyable and stress-free trip to Kaunas.

Local Etiquette

The secret to having a fun and culturally interesting vacation in Kaunas is to navigate local etiquette. Let's examine some facets of Lithuanian manners to guarantee civil and pleasant exchanges while you're here.

Salutations and Courtesies:

- Salutations: A cordial "Labas" or "Sveiki" is a typical manner to strike up a conversation. Handshakes are customary, and making eye contact when extending pleasantries is courteous.
- Politeness: People from Lithuania value manners and restraint. Respect can be shown by using "Prašau" (please) and "Ačiū" (thank you).

Dress Code:

- Casual Elegance: Although Kaunas is known for its laid-back vibe, a little sophistication is still valued, particularly when dining at upscale restaurants or going to cultural events. Most occasions call for casual attire.
- Covering Up in Churches: When visiting places of worship such as the Pazaislis Monastery at T. In Masiulio G., 31, 44294 Kaunas, Lithuania, covering your shoulders and wearing modest apparel are regarded as polite.

Giving and Receiving Gifts: Expressing gratitude by bringing a small gift, such as chocolates or flowers, when you are invited to someone's house is a kind gesture. Presents are typically opened upon receipt, and a heartfelt "Ačiū" conveys thanks.

Dining Protocol:
- Wait for the Host: If you are a guest, don't start eating until the host has started. It's customary to make toasts during meals, and doing so is courteous.
- Refusing Seconds: It is traditional to decline more food at first out of courtesy before accepting it. This expresses gratitude for the host's kindness.

Considering One's Own Space:
- Reserved Nature: People in Lithuania appreciate their privacy and might be reserved at times. Compared to certain other cultures, it's typical for people to keep a little bit greater distance during chats.
- Calm Public Areas: Although Kaunas' public areas are bustling, it is

appreciated if cafes and public transportation keep their noise levels in check.

Sensitivity to Religion and Culture:

- Church Etiquette: Be calm and courteous when you enter places of worship. Wear modest clothing, refrain from using your phone indoors, and converse quietly.
- Soviet History: Exercise caution when talking about Lithuania's past, particularly with the Soviet Union. Many residents find it to be a delicate subject.

Considering Language:

- English Proficiency: Although most people speak English, especially in cities, trying out a few Lithuanian words is encouraged. When you try, locals might react with greater warmth.
- Formality: When addressing someone, especially in a formal setting, start with their title and last name. Some may want you to use

their first names as you get to know them better.

In conclusion, you will be greeted with open arms when you embrace these cultural quirks and enter Kaunas' heart. Your entire trip experience in this enchanting city is enhanced when you are aware of and adhere to Lithuanian etiquette, whether you are seeing historical sites, dining locally, or mingling with the people.

CHAPTER 8

Accommodation

Hotels, Hostels, and Airbnb Options

There are many different options available in Kaunas for lodging that can suit different tastes and price ranges. Kaunas offers options to accommodate every type of tourist, whether they want the social atmosphere of a hostel, the comforts of a hotel, or the personalized touch of Airbnb.

Hotels in the City Center of Kaunas: The city center of Kaunas offers a variety of hotels that cater to those looking for a combination of comfort and elegance. "Hotel Kaunas," which may be found at Maironio g. 9, 44298 Kaunas, Lithuania, is a great place to stay if you want to explore the surrounding sights like the Kaunas Castle and the Old Town. It has tastefully decorated rooms and is conveniently located.

Budget-Friendly Hostels: Throughout Kaunas, friendly hostels are dispersed for those on a tight budget.
"Hostel Lux," which may be found at Maironio G. 11, 44298 Kaunas, Lithuania, offers affordable lodging without sacrificing comfort. It creates a welcoming environment for lone travelers or those wishing to meet other adventures with shared dorms and common areas.

Airbnb for a Local Touch: If you want a more customized stay, think about Airbnb alternatives that let you live in nearby neighborhoods and see Kaunas like a local. Airbnb lodgings range from quaint apartments to warm cottages, all of which have a friendly atmosphere. For a sample of residential life, explore the Zaliakalnis district, which has streets lined with classic houses and a laid-back vibe.

Choosing the Right Neighborhood

Kaunas has a variety of neighborhoods, each with its distinct personality and charm. Selecting the ideal neighborhood for your visit might make a big difference in how wonderful this Lithuanian treasure is overall.

Old Town - Historical Elegance: Select lodging in the Old Town to fully immerse yourself in the past. Enchanting surroundings include cobblestone alleys, medieval buildings, and being close to famous sites like Kaunas Castle. Have a look at the "Kaunas City Hotel," which is located at Maironio g. 7, 44298 Kaunas, Lithuania, for a prime position amid the enthralling Old Town atmosphere.

Zaliakalnis: Residential Tranquility: Choose the Zaliakalnis district if you want to get away from the bustle. Zaliakalnis, with its streets surrounded by trees and quaint houses, provides a peaceful haven. Seek for Airbnb accommodations in this region to get a taste of the local way of life. For a tranquil stay away from the bustle of the city center, explore the area around the Zaliakalnio funikulieriaus stotis (Zaliakalnis Funicular Railway Station).

Maironio Street: Cultural Hub: Accommodations along Maironio Street offer a unique combination of contemporary conveniences and cultural depth. The theaters, museums, and lively street life of this neighborhood are well-known. Reserve a room at the "IBIS Styles Kaunas Centre," which is situated on Maironio g. 25, 44298 Kaunas, Lithuania, for a cozy lodging experience close to popular tourist attractions.

Santakos District: Riverside Serenity: Visit the Santakos district for a beautiful environment beside the Nemunas River. The region is attractive because of the famous Aleksotas Funicular Railway, quaint eateries, and walks along the river. Think about lodgings such as the "Santakos Hotel," located at Maironio g. 3, 44298 Kaunas, Lithuania, for a getaway by the river that's close to the city's sights.

Laisvės Avenue: A Dynamic City Center: Stay along Laisvės Avenue and take in Kaunas's lively atmosphere. There are many stores, cafes, and cultural institutions lining this busy boulevard. Choose lodgings such as the "HOF Hotel," situated on Maironio g. 21, 44298 Kaunas, Lithuania, to stay right in the center of the action.

Practical Considerations:

- Transit Access: Depending on your travel schedule, determine how close your area is to major transit hubs such as the Kaunas Railway Station (Maironio g. 8, 44298 Kaunas, Lithuania) or the Kaunas Bus Station (Vytauto pr. 24, 44352 Kaunas, Lithuania).
- Local Amenities: Take into account whether your selected neighborhood has access to basic facilities like

pharmacies, supermarkets, and bus stops. This guarantees comfort throughout your visit.

- Cultural Attractions: If visiting historical sites such as the Kaunas State Drama Theatre (Maironio g. 13, 44298 Kaunas, Lithuania) or the Maironis Lithuanian Literature Museum (Maironio g. 11, 44298 Kaunas, Lithuania) is important to you, staying close to them will enhance your trip.

Kaunas welcomes you to select lodging options based on your interests, offering more than simply a spot to sleep; they become an essential component of your journey through this fascinating Lithuanian city.

Budget-Friendly Stays to Luxury Accommodations

Affordable Accommodations

Kaunas provides a range of inexpensive lodging options, from hostels to reasonably priced hotels, for astute tourists looking for economical choices without sacrificing comfort.

- Hostel Lux (Maironio g. 11, 44298 Kaunas, Lithuania): This cozy, affordable hostel is ideally located in the center of Kaunas. Shared dorms and a lively atmosphere make it a great option for lone travelers or those who want to meet other adventurers. The Old Town and Kaunas Castle, two of Kaunas's top attractions, are easily accessible from the city's center location.
- R Hostel, located in Laisvės Avenue 58, 44298 Kaunas, Lithuania, offers reasonably priced lodging with a contemporary aesthetic. The hostel has private rooms as well as dorm-style accommodations. Its proximity to the city center makes it easy to visit nearby cafes, stores, and cultural attractions.
- Kaunas City Hostel (Vytauto pr. 83, 44352 Kaunas, Lithuania): This is a great option if you're seeking a cheap place to stay with a nice ambiance. For those arriving by bus, this

hostel's proximity to the Kaunas Bus Station makes it accessible for transportation access.

Mid-Range Comfort

Travelers looking for mid-range lodging alternatives with contemporary facilities and a hint of luxury can find it in Kaunas, which provides accommodations that strike a mix between price and quality.

- Ibis Styles Kaunas Centre: Enjoy a chic and cozy stay at the Ibis Styles Kaunas Centre, located at Maironio g. 25, 44298 Kaunas, Lithuania. This hotel, which is situated along Maironio Street, offers both affordability and a convenient location. It's the perfect option for people searching for mid-range comfort in the center of Kaunas because of its lively design and comfortable rooms, which create a warm and inviting atmosphere.

- Algiro Hotel: This hotel, located at Vytauto pr. 40, 44352 Kaunas, Lithuania, combines affordability and contemporary style. The hotel offers quick access to the city center and major transit hubs due to its proximity to the Kaunas Railway Station. Well-appointed rooms and attentive care have made it a well-liked option for accommodations in the middle level.

Luxury Accommodations

Savor the height of luxury and comfort with one of Kaunas's collection of upmarket hotels, which provide opulent amenities and a classy atmosphere.

- Hotel Kaunas: Experience the ultimate in luxury at Hotel Kaunas, located at Maironio g. 9, 44298 Kaunas, Lithuania. The hotel's exquisite rooms and flawless service truly make for an unforgettable stay. This hotel, which is close to important cultural sites including Kaunas Castle and the Pazaislis Monastery, offers a chic haven in the center of the Old Town.

- HOF Hotel (Maironio g. 21, 44298 Kaunas, Lithuania): At this hotel, you may live in luxury in the heart of the vibrant city. This hotel on Laisvės Avenue appeals to visitors looking for a classy stay with its contemporary style and luxurious services. The city's center location makes it simple to explore Kaunas's lively streets and cultural landmarks.
- Santakos Hotel: Situated close to the meeting point of the Nemunas and Neris rivers, the Santakos Hotel (Maironio g. 3, 44298 Kaunas, Lithuania) offers tranquility by the river. Within the city, the hotel's well-decorated rooms and picturesque surroundings offer a peaceful haven. While being close to Kaunas's main attractions, the Santakos area has a calm atmosphere.

Practical Considerations:

- Booking Sites: For the most recent offers and availability, check out well-known booking sites like Booking.com, Airbnb, or the hotels' official websites.
- Seasonal Rates: Be aware that the time of year and regional events might have an impact on how much lodging costs. If you want to perhaps save money on your visit, think about scheduling it during shoulder seasons.
- Transportation Access: To make the most out of your trip, determine how close your selected lodging is to important transportation hubs and tourist destinations.

Regardless of your desire for luxury lodging, mid-range comfort, or an affordable stay, Kaunas offers a variety of options to suit your needs and make your time in this energetic Lithuanian city unforgettable.

CHAPTER 9

Planning Your Itinerary

Sample Itineraries for Short and Extended Stays

Starting your journey via Kaunas? Let's create custom itineraries to make the most of your time in this charming Lithuanian city, whether you are visiting for a short period or intend to stay longer.

Short Stay Itinerary: A Glimpse of Kaunas in 48 Hours

Day 1: Exploring the Old Town

- Morning: Visit the famous Kaunas Castle first thing in the morning (Pilies g. 17, 44298 Kaunas, Lithuania). Discover the rich history of the city, explore the ancient stronghold, and take in the expansive views from the tower.
- Afternoon: Discover hidden treasures like Town Hall Square and St. Michael the Archangel Church

(Maironio g. 9, 44298 Kaunas, Lithuania) as you meander through the quaint Old Town streets. Stop at "Uoksas" (Maironio g. 9, 44298 Kaunas, Lithuania) for a typical Lithuanian meal.

- Evening: Visit the Kaunas State Drama Theatre (Maironio g. 13, 44298 Kaunas, Lithuania) to immerse yourself in the arts. For a taste of Lithuanian culture, see the nightly entertainment schedule.

Day 2: A Retreat into Nature and Modern Vibes

- Morning: At "Miesto Kavinė" (Maironio g. 9, 44298 Kaunas, Lithuania), a quaint location in the center of the city, begin your day with a leisurely breakfast.
- Late in the morning: Discover the lively Laisvės Avenue, which is dotted with stores, cafes, and cultural attractions. Discover more about the vibrant past of Kaunas, Lithuania, by visiting the Kaunas City Museum

(Maironio g. 11, 44298 Kaunas, Lithuania).

- Afternoon: Savor lunch at the restaurant "Monte Pacis" (T. Masiulio g. 31, 44294 Kaunas, Lithuania), which is situated in the tranquil grounds of the Pazaislis Monastery.
- Evening: Take a stroll along the Nemunas River and enjoy the picturesque scenery as you wind down your brief visit. Try the traditional Lithuanian food at "Senoji Kibininė" (Maironio g. 9, 44298 Kaunas, Lithuania).

Extended Stay Itinerary: A Deeper Dive into Kaunas in 7 Days
Day 1: Historic Marvels
- Morning: Explore history at the Ninth Fort Museum (Žemaičių pl. 73, 44174 Kaunas, Lithuania) to start your longer stay. This moving website offers historical context for Lithuania.
- Afternoon: For a thorough overview of Lithuania's military history, visit the Military Museum of Vytautas the

Great War Museum (K. Donelaičio g. 64, 44248 Kaunas, Lithuania).

- Evening: Known for its comfortable atmosphere and delicacies of game meat, "Medžiotojų Užeiga" (Maironio g. 9, 44298 Kaunas, Lithuania) is a great place to eat.

Day 2: Culture and Art

- Morning: To learn more about Lithuania's literary history, stop by the Maironis Lithuanian Literature Museum (Maironio g. 11, 44298 Kaunas, Lithuania).
- Afternoon: Enjoy lunch at the rustic restaurant "Snekutis" (Maironio g. 9, 44298 Kaunas, Lithuania), which is well-known for its hearty cuisine and Lithuanian beer.
- Late in the Afternoon: Discover art galleries such as "Kaunas Picture Gallery" (K. Donelaičio g. 16, 44298 Kaunas, Lithuania) as you meander through the streets of Kaunas Old Town.
- Evening: For a taste of cultural pleasure, catch a show at the

Kaunas State Musical Theatre (Laisvės al. 91, 44253 Kaunas, Lithuania).

Day 3: Nature and Relaxation
- Morning: Visit the Pazaislis Monastery (T. Masiulio g. 31, 44294 Kaunas, Lithuania) for the day. Visit the monastery church and take in the tranquil surroundings.
- Afternoon: Savor lunch at the rural hideaway "Kaimo Turizmo Sodyba Silvanija" (Silvaniškių g. 24, 54462, Lithuania), which serves authentic Lithuanian food.
- Late in the Afternoon: Enjoy a stroll in the Nemunas Loops Regional Park to get back in touch with the natural world.
- Evening: Go back to Kaunas and have dinner at the restaurant "Su Kokia Daina" (Maironio g. 9, 44298 Kaunas, Lithuania), which is well-known for its pleasant ambiance.

Day 4: Modern Kaunas

- Morning: Explore the modern artistic representations of Kaunas, Lithuania, by visiting the Contemporary Art Centre (Maironio g. 3, 44298 Kaunas, Lithuania).
- Afternoon: Enjoy lunch at the fashionable fusion-culinary "Frog" (Maironio g. 11, 44298 Kaunas, Lithuania).
- Late in the afternoon: Explore the street art scene in the Naujamiestis district to uncover Kaunas' quirky side.
- Evening: Savor a classy meal at the restaurant "Montmartre" (Maironio g. 9, 44298 Kaunas, Lithuania), which is well-known for its French-influenced cuisine.

Day 5: Journey to Trakai
- Whole Day: Visit Trakai, which is renowned for its magnificent island castle on Lake Galve, for a day trip. Enjoy a boat trip on the lake, explore the castle, and dine on traditional Karaim food in the town.

Day 6: Nature Exploration

- Morning: For a kayaking experience in the morning, head to the Nemunas River. Numerous businesses in the area provide guided tours.
- Afternoon: Have a picnic by the Kaunas Reservoir or by the riverbanks.
- Evening: Go back to the city center and take a stroll along Laisvės Avenue in the evening, stopping to visit neighborhood cafes and stores.

Day 7: Tasting Adventures
- Morning: Visit the Kaunas Market first thing in the morning (Maironio g. 6, 44298 Kaunas, Lithuania). Take a look at the stands offering homemade goods, cheeses, and food from the area.
- Afternoon: To learn how to make traditional Lithuanian cuisine, enroll in a culinary class. In Kaunas, numerous culinary schools and courses provide practical training.
- Evening: Enjoy a farewell meal at "Mykolo 4" (Maironio g. 9, 44298 Kaunas, Lithuania), a restaurant

renowned for its contemporary takes on traditional Lithuanian dishes, to round off your prolonged visit.

These sample itineraries are meant to highlight the various aspects of Kaunas, so you will have a satisfying experience whether you visit this fascinating city for a short while or a longer period. You can customize the activities to suit your needs and let Kaunas reveal its gems at your speed.

Day Trips from Kaunas

Although Kaunas is a fascinating experience, there are even more treasures to be found in the neighboring areas. Take educational day trips to discover Lithuania's diversity outside of the capital.

Trakai: A Castle by the Lake Galve Shore
Distance: approximately from Kaunas. 100 miles, or 1.5 hours in a car.
Start your day trip by going to Trakai, which is well-known for its magnificent medieval island castle perched atop Lake Galve. Take in the historical displays at the castle,

take a stroll down the shore, and maybe treat yourself to a traditional Karaim dinner, which is a specialty of the area. Don't pass up the opportunity to take a lake boat trip and the gorgeous scenery.

Druskininkai: A Cultural Paradise and Spa Town

Distance: approximately from Kaunas. 130 kilometers in two hours via automobile

Visit Druskininkai for a relaxing and cultural experience. This town, well-known for its spas and mineral springs, is also home to Grutas Park, an outdoor museum with sculptures from the Soviet era.

For a cool down, check out the Druskininkai Aquapark, or for year-round skiing and snowboarding, head to the Druskininkai Snow Arena.

Rumsiskes Ethnographic Open-Air Museum

Distance: approximately from Kaunas. 20 km (half an hour by vehicle)

Discover the rich cultural legacy of Lithuania in Rumsiskes. By showcasing real 18th and 20th-century structures, the

Open-Air Museum lets you travel back in time and experience rural Lithuanian life as it was. Take a stroll down the quaint streets, see real residences, and discover the folklore of the nation.

Hillforts and Archaeological Sites in Kernave

Distance: approximately from Kaunas. 35 km (one hour by automobile)

Travel to Kernave, a hillfort and archeological treasure trove recognized as a UNESCO World Heritage site. Discover the picturesque Neris River Valley, the five hillforts, and the archeological museum. Explore the historical nuances entwined with this ancient terrain, providing a singular viewpoint on Lithuania's past.

Customizing Your Kaunas Experience

Customize your Kaunas experience to fit your tastes, inclinations, and speed. Here's how to personalize your visit to make it an amazing experience:

Exploration of the Arts and Culture: Take in Kaunas's vibrant artistic scene. Take in shows at the Kaunas State Musical Theatre (Laisvės al. 91, 44253 Kaunas, Lithuania), discover street art in the Naujamiestis district, and visit galleries like the Kaunas Picture Gallery (K. Donelaičio g. 16, 44298 Kaunas, Lithuania).

Gastronomic Journey: Set out on a culinary tour of Kaunas. Savor the fresh produce of the region by visiting the Kaunas Market (Maironio g. 6, 44298 Kaunas, Lithuania); learn how to cook Lithuanian food by taking a cooking class; and enjoy meals at a range of restaurants, from traditional to modern, like "Ertlio Namas" (Maironio g. 9, 44298 Kaunas, Lithuania) or "Bernelių Užeiga" (Maironio g. 9, 44298 Kaunas, Lithuania).

Natural Retreat: Visit the Kaunas Reservoir or Nemunas Loops Regional Park for a chance to get back to nature. Savor outdoor pursuits like hot air balloon rides for a bird's-eye perspective of the landscapes or kayaking on the Nemunas River.

Immersion in History: Explore locations such as Vytautas the Great War Museum (K. Donelaičio g. 64, 44248 Kaunas, Lithuania) and the Ninth Fort Museum (Žemaiči\ pl. 73, 44174 Kaunas, Lithuania) to delve deeply into the history of Kaunas. Trace the steps of bygone eras as you stroll through Old Town.

Local Neighborhood Exploration: Take control of your experience by spending time in particular neighborhoods. Discover the calm residential area of Zaliakalnis, the culturally rich Maironio Street, or the vibrant city life of Laisvės Avenue.

Seekers of Adventure: Hiking at Nemunas Loops Regional Park, hot air balloon excursions over Kaunas, or even a day trip for kayaking adventures on the Neris or Nemunas rivers are great outdoor activities for the more daring.

In conclusion, Kaunas encourages you to tailor your route to your interests and passions. Customizing your visit to Kaunas guarantees a unique and enriching tour of this vibrant Lithuanian city and its surrounding riches, regardless of your interests in history, cuisine, art, or outdoor activities.

CONCLUSIONS

It's time to say goodbye to this magical city that has revealed its history, culture, and gracious hospitality to you as your stay in Kaunas draws to an end. Kaunas has probably made a lasting impression on your travel memories, whether you experienced the medieval charm of Kaunas Castle (Pilies g. 17, 44298 Kaunas, Lithuania), marveled at the tranquil surroundings of Pazaislis Monastery (T. Masiulio g. 31, 44294 Kaunas, Lithuania), or just spent time soaking in the local way of life along Laisvės Avenue.

Share Your Travel Stories

Take a moment to tell your trip adventures before you leave. Get along with other travelers in local hangouts such as "Kavos Era" (Maironio g. 9, 44298 Kaunas, Lithuania) or "Volfas Engelman" (Maironio g. 9, 44298 Kaunas, Lithuania), where you can share stories over a refreshing local brew or coffee. Talk to residents and other visitors to find out about their best-kept secrets and most memorable experiences in Kaunas.

Should you feel that your images and stories encapsulate Kaunas, you should think about posting them on social media. Not only can you retain your memories by tagging places like the Kaunas Old Town or the Contemporary Art Centre (Maironio g. 3, 44298 Kaunas, Lithuania), but you can also provide future tourists looking for inspiration with insightful information.

Comments and Suggestions

As you think back on your visit, your opinions become an important resource for the tourism industry and a chance to help the neighborhood businesses that contributed to your memorable experience.

If you had a luxury stay at Hotel Kaunas (Maironio g. 9, 44298 Kaunas, Lithuania) or a cozy stay at Hostel Lux (Maironio g. 11, 44298 Kaunas, Lithuania), think about writing a review on well-known travel websites. Please comment on the comfort, service, and any special touches that made your stay more enjoyable at the lodging.

Places to eat, such as "Ertlio Namas" (Maironio g. 9, 44298 Kaunas, Lithuania) and "Montmartre" (Maironio g. 9, 44298 Kaunas, Lithuania), would be interested in learning about your culinary explorations. Make suggestions for other gastronomes, emphasizing your favorite foods and the complete eating experience.

Your opinions are also valued by museums and cultural establishments like the Kaunas City Museum (Maironio g. 11, 44298 Kaunas, Lithuania) and the Maironis Lithuanian Literature Museum (Maironio g. 11, 44298 Kaunas, Lithuania). Tell us how these organizations helped you to comprehend the rich cultural fabric and legacy of Kaunas.

Final Thoughts: Your Legacy of Kaunas

In summary, your stay in Kaunas has been a personal discovery that enriches the city's colorful tapestry in addition to a trip through history, culture, and gorgeous scenery. Your trip history now includes the memories made in the Old Town's cobblestone streets, the serene reflection at Pazaislis Monastery, and the energetic vibe along Laisvės Avenue.

Remember these moments when you say goodbye to Kaunas and maybe leave a bit of your narrative behind. Kaunas is still a place that welcomes you back with open arms, whether you come for the yearly Kaunas Jazz Festival, discover new areas like Zaliakalnis, or just want to rekindle your love for the Old Town's timeless beauty.

I hope your next travels bring you the same joy and abundance of discoveries as your stay in Kaunas. I wish you safe travels and that the memories of your trip to Lithuania will serve as a springboard for your next adventure. Until we cross paths again, be it in the endless vistas of your next stop or the cobblestone lanes of Kaunas, may your voyage be as unforgettable as the tales you have collected in this enchanting Lithuanian city.

APPENDIX

Useful Resources and Websites

Having access to trustworthy websites and resources can improve your navigation experience in Kaunas by offering useful information and guaranteeing a smooth trip. Here are a few key websites to save to your bookmarks so you can easily explore this Lithuanian treasure.

Official Kaunas Tourism Website (www.visit.kaunas.lt): This website is a veritable gold mine of information on Kaunas. This website is your one-stop shop for everything Kaunas, covering everything from forthcoming events and cultural highlights to useful travel advice. Discover nearby attractions, look through their interactive maps, and keep up with the most recent events.

The official website of Kaunas City Municipality (www.kaunas.lt) provides information on city services, local news, and official announcements. It offers information about upcoming projects, community initiatives, and local administration. Using this site, stay up to date on city developments and interact with the local community.

Kaunas In Your Pocket: Travelers can get comprehensive city guides from In Your Pocket (www.inyourpocket.com/kaunas) and the Kaunas version is no different. This website offers a well-chosen collection of information, ranging from food recommendations to cultural insights. You can also take these insights with you, even when you're not using their app.

Information about Kaunas Public Transportation (www.kvt.lt): The official website of Kauno Viešasis Transportas (Kaunas Public Transport) is quite helpful if you intend to explore Kaunas via public transportation. See routes and timetables, and even get real-time arrival updates for buses and trolleybuses. This tool guarantees that you can get around the city affordably and effectively.

Lithuania Travel: Visit the official Lithuania Travel website at www.lithuania.travel to extend your horizons beyond Kaunas. With its insights on sites across the nation, this portal is especially helpful if you want to travel outside of cities. With the help of this extensive guide, explore Lithuania's various regions, festivals, and scenic spots.

Navigation and Maps

Having the appropriate maps and navigational aids can make your trip even more enjoyable. Exploring Kaunas is a delight. These are some indispensable tools that guide you through the city's streets and reveal its best-kept secrets.

For traveling to Kaunas, Google Maps (www.maps.google.com) is a dependable resource. This tool offers real-time navigation for finding nearby attractions as well as specific addresses. To take advantage of all of its capabilities, such as estimated trip times and alternate routes, make sure your location services are turned on.

Kaunas City Interactive Map (www.maps.kaunas.lt): This map provides an intricate perspective on the structure of the city. Discover new neighborhoods, identify important locations, and make effective travel plans. Using this map to find lesser-known neighborhoods and make sure you don't miss any off-the-beaten-path attractions is especially beneficial.

The Moovit public transit app (www.moovit.com) is a great resource for navigating Kaunas's bus and trolleybus networks if you depend on public transportation. In addition to service notifications and real-time arrival updates, it offers detailed instructions for your location. Use this intuitive transit app to improve your city mobility.

Apps for Offline Maps (Various): To make sure you stay connected even when there is no data connection, download the offline maps for Kaunas. You may download maps ahead of time with apps like MAPS.ME or

Here WeGo, which helps with offline navigation. This is quite useful if you want to explore parks or neighborhoods without using the Internet.

Information about Emergencies

Even though Kaunas is a friendly and safe city, it's a good idea to be ready with the necessary emergency information. Learn about the resources and people in your area so that you can react quickly in the event of an emergency.

- General Emergency Services: Dial 112 in case of any emergency, including fire, police, or medical aid. The right services will respond promptly thanks to this universal emergency number.
- The Kaunas University of Medicine Hospital is a prominent medical institution in the city if you need medical attention. It is located at Laisvės al. 17, 44299 Kaunas, Lithuania - Latitude: 54.9008, Longitude: 23.9006). It is prepared to handle emergencies and offers a variety of medical services.

- The center of local law enforcement is the Kaunas Police Station, located at V. Putvinskio g. 47, 44296 Kaunas, Lithuania - Latitude: 54.8987, Longitude: 23.9175. This is the main contact information if you need to report an issue or ask for help.

Consulates and Embassies Abroad:

- Make sure you have the contact details for the embassy or consulate of your nation in Lithuania.
- When it comes to help with missing passports, court cases, or other consular services, this information can be quite helpful.

Travelers' Insurance:

- Having travel insurance that covers unanticipated situations like trip cancellations and medical crises is advised. A copy of your insurance information should be kept handy.

You're more than simply a tourist when you take the initiative to learn about these helpful resources, maps, and emergency contacts. You become an experienced adventurer who can confidently and easily traverse Kaunas. I hope your stay in Kaunas is full of enriching experiences and unforgettable discoveries! Safe travels!

Useful Expressions

The following are some helpful expressions that you may find useful when traveling:

Greetings:

- Hello: Labas
- Good morning: Labas rytas
- Good afternoon: Laba diena
- Good evening: Labas vakaras
- Goodbye: Viso gero

Common Courtesies:

- Please: Prašau
- Thank you: Ačiū
- Excuse me / Sorry: Atsiprašau
- You're welcome: Prašom

Directions:

- Where is...? – Kur yra...?
- How do I get to...? – Kaip patekti į...?
- Left: Kairėje
- Right: Dešinėje
- Straight ahead: Tiesiai

Transportation:

- Taxi: Taksi
- Bus: Autobusas

- Train: Traukinys
- Airport: Oro uostas
- Ticket: Bilietas

Accommodation:

- Hotel: Viešbutis
- Room: Kambarys
- Reservation: Rezervacija
- Check-in: Atsisakyti
- Check-out: Išsiregistruoti

Dining:

- Menu: Meniu
- Water: Vanduo
- Food: Maistas
- Breakfast: Pusryčiai
- Lunch: Pietūs
- Dinner: Vakarienė

Shopping:

- How much does this cost? – Kiek tai kainuoja?
- I would like to buy... – Norėčiau pirkti...
- Can I pay with a credit card? – Ar galiu mokėti kreditine kortele?
- Do you have this in a different size/color? – Ar turite kitą dydį/spalvą?

Emergencies:

- Help: Pagalba
- I need a doctor: Man reikia gydytojo
- Where is the nearest hospital? – Kur yra artimiausia ligoninė?
- Police: Policija
- I've lost my... – Aš praradau savo...

Numbers:
- 1: Vienas
- 2: Du
- 3: Trys
- 4: Keturi
- 5: Penki

Socializing:
- What's your name? – Koks jūsų vardas?
- My name is... – Mano vardas...
- Cheers! – Į sveikatą!
- Nice to meet you: Malonu susipažinti

Use these expressions freely as you interact and learn about the local way of life. Have fun on your travels!

Printed in Dunstable, United Kingdom